TH

PROJECT

A Case of Mistaken Identity

A SELF-COACHING BIBLE STUDY
COURSE TO DEVELOP A STRONG
SENSE OF SELF-IDENTITY IN
CHRIST

BY

ALLEN MCCRAY

Lifeimpactllc.com

The Identity Project: A Case of Mistaken Identity

Copyright © 2015 Life Impact LLC

Table of Contents

INTRODUCTION:

The goal of this self-directed study is to assist in creating a healthy image of God, as well as yourself. When you discover your identity in Christ and align yourself with His thoughts toward you, you will be energized, inspired, and empowered.

It's in Christ that we find out who we are and what we are living for. Long before we first heard of Christ and got our hopes up, he had his eye on us, had designs on us for glorious living, part of the overall purpose he is working out in everything and everyone. (Ephesians 1:11-12: The Message)

"The two most important beliefs we have are what we believe about God and what we believe about ourselves." Pastor Michael Maiden

If we get our image of Him right, we will get the right image of ourselves.

CHAPTER 1

A Case of Mistaken Identity

What is your earliest memory of God? How did you picture Him in your mind? My first image of God was a big eyeball in the sky. Where did I get such a picture of him? From my early Sunday school teaching. We used to sing a song that went something like this:

"There is an all-seeing eye watching you... little hands watch what you do...little feet watch where you go...little eyes watch what you see... little mouth watch what you say...There's an all-seeing eye watching you. " Is there any wonder that I would have such a mistaken identity of God? And, I was pretty sure He was angry and out to get me.

When I ask this question about people's first image of God, I have gotten interesting answers. "He is an old man sitting on a big throne." "He is an angry grandfather who disapproves of me." One pastor's wife said, "He looks like the picture on the baking soda box, a big bicep with a hammer in His hand, ready to smash me." I have gotten a few positive responses such as a kind old man, a loving old man. It's interesting that none of these line up with what the Bible says about God.

Take a moment and reflect back to your first impression or image of God. Was it positive or negative? Use the space below to write about that image or draw a picture of that image.

_____

_____

_____

_____

_____

_____

Now, ask yourself this question: where did I get that image?

_____

_____

_____

_____

_____

How does this image of God impact my relationship with him?

_____

_____

_____

_____

_____

An unhealthy image of God produces an unhealthy image of self.

Another case of mistaken identity

13 When Jesus came into the region of Caesarea Philippi, He asked His disciples, saying, "Who do men say that I, the Son of Man, am?"

14 So they said, "Some say John the Baptist, some Elijah, and others Jeremiah or one of the prophets."

15 He said to them, "But who do you say that I am?"

16 Simon Peter answered and said, "You are the Christ, the Son of the living God."

17 Jesus answered and said to him, "Blessed are you, Simon Bar-Jonah, for flesh and blood has not revealed this to you, but My Father who is in heaven. 18 And I also say to you that you are Peter, and on this rock I will build My church, and the gates of Hades shall not prevail against it. 19 And I will give you the keys of the kingdom of heaven, and whatever you bind on earth will be bound in heaven, and whatever you loose on earth will be loosed in heaven." (Matthew 16:13-19 NKJ)

It's easy to get caught up in identifying God with what is familiar to us. In the time that

Jesus was on the earth, John the Baptist, Elijah, Jeremiah and the prophets were familiar to the religious people. Therefore, that is how they wanted to identify Christ. Today, people often make the same mistake by identifying God with what is familiar to them. God and the church, as we know it, become one and the same. This may surprise you, but God is not a Baptist or a Pentecostal. He is not a Catholic or any other *flavor* of our Christian culture. He is not identified as a Christian. My point is, He is not a religion. God is love. Jesus was the personification of God—God in the flesh. The identity that we get of Jesus in the church is, too often, different than the identity we get from the Bible. Man often recreates God into his image.

In the Gospel of Luke, Jesus gives us three different pictures of God the Father to help us know Him. At that time, the prevailing image of God was that He hated sinners and took pleasure in their demise. Jesus painted a different picture by telling the story of the Lost Sheep, the Lost Coin and the most popular story, the lost or prodigal son. In each of these stories, God rejoices over the lost being found; just as He rejoices today over every person who comes to know and experience the saving grace of Jesus Christ.

First Story, the lost sheep:

15 Then all the tax collectors and the sinners drew near to Him to hear Him. 2 And the Pharisees and scribes complained, saying, "This Man receives sinners and eats with them." 3 So He spoke this parable to them, saying:

4 "What man of you, having a hundred sheep, if he loses one of them, does not leave the ninety-nine in the wilderness, and go after the one which is lost until he finds it? 5 And when he has found it, he lays it on his shoulders, rejoicing. 6 And when he comes home, he calls together his friends and neighbors, saying to them, 'Rejoice with me, for I have found my sheep which was lost!' 7 I say to you that likewise there will be more joy in heaven over one sinner who repents than over ninety-nine just persons who need no repentance.

What was your first impression about the lost sheep? Did you make any judgments about it, such as: was it a bad sheep, young sheep, etc.? Write your thoughts in the space below. Can you identify a time in your life when you may have been the "lost sheep?"

_____

_____

_____

_____

_____

_____

_____

_____

The second story, the Lost Coin

8 "Or what woman, having ten silver coins, if she loses one coin, does not light a lamp, sweep the house, and search carefully until she finds it? 9 And when she has found it, she calls her friends and neighbors together, saying, 'Rejoice with me, for I have found the piece which I lost!' 10 Likewise, I say to you, there is joy in the presence of the angels of God over one sinner who repents."

Please notice the story doesn't tell us *how* she lost the coin, only that she lost the coin. It has been suggested that the coin had more than monetary value; it may have been part of her dowry. The indication is, that it was part of her identity.

Did you have any thoughts about the woman losing the coin? Take a moment and write any impression you might have had.

_____

_____

_____

_____

_____

Can you think of a time when you may have lost part of yourself by violating one of your values, and—like the woman—you lost a piece of yourself.

_____

_____

_____

_____

_____

What steps are you willing to take to reclaim that part of your identity?

_____

_____

_____

_____

_____

The third story: The lost son:

11 Then He said: "A certain man had two sons. 12 And the younger of them said to his father, 'Father, give me the portion of goods that falls to me.' So he divided to them his livelihood. 13 And not many days after, the younger son gathered all together, journeyed to a far country, and there wasted his possessions with prodigal living. 14 But when he had spent all, there arose a severe famine in that land, and he began to be in want. 15 Then he went and joined himself to a citizen of that country, and he sent him into his fields to feed swine. 16 And he would gladly have filled his stomach with the pods that the swine ate, and no one gave him anything.

17 "But when he came to himself, he said, 'How many of my father's hired servants have bread enough and to spare, and I perish with hunger! 18 I will arise and go to my father, and will say to him, "Father, I have sinned against heaven and before you, 19, and I am no longer worthy to be called your son. Make me like one of your hired servants."'

20 "And he arose and came to his father. But when he was still a great way off, his father saw him and had compassion, and ran and fell on his neck and kissed him. 21 And the son said to him, 'Father, I have sinned against heaven and in your sight, and am no longer worthy to be called your son.'

22 "But the father said to his servants, 'Bring out the best robe and put it on him, and put a ring on his hand and sandals on his feet. 23 And bring the fatted calf here and kill it, and let us eat and be merry; 24 for this my son was dead and is alive again; he was lost and is found.' And they began to be merry. (Luke 15:1-24 NKJV)

What was your first impression of the son?

_____

_____

_____

_____

_____

Can you identify a time when you made a similar choice that left you feeling undeserving?

_____

_____

_____

_____

_____

_____

_____

How can the image of a God, that rejoices over what was lost and is found, impact your life?

_____

_____

_____

_____

_____

Is the image of God as a loving, forgiving, rejoicing father different from your childhood or current image of God? If so how?

_____

_____

_____

_____

_____

_____

_____

_____

_____

CHAPTER 2

A Case of Identity Theft

If what you have been taught about God creates an identity that you are small, insignificant, and sentenced to live your life in the prison of shame, guilt, and condemnation, you are the victim of identity theft.

As the lost son planned to return to his father's house, he looked at himself through the lens of guilt, shame, and condemnation, which stole his true identity, causing him to create a false identity.

"I will arise and go to my father, and will say to him, "Father, I have sinned against heaven and before you, and I am no longer worthy to be called your son. Make me like one of your hired servants."

His false image required him to describe his relationship with his father as a hired servant with no access to his father's provisions, blessings, and authority. However, the father could only see him through the lens of son-ship and couldn't wait to restore his true identity.

How do you describe your relationship with God?

_____

_____

_____

_____

_____

How would you like your relationship with God to be different?

_____

_____

_____

_____

_____

What would have to change for you to have the relationship you want with God?

_____

_____

_____

_____

_____

If you had the relationship you want with God, how would your life be different?

_____

_____

_____

_____

_____

What steps would you like to take to allow God to restore your relationship with him?

_____

_____

_____

_____

_____

As the victim of identity theft, you—like the lost son—may have made up a false identity, which becomes a stumbling block to your faith and keeps you from receiving the very things that you are requesting. This fabricated concept of self, in relationship to God, puts you in a state of spiritual coma, anesthetized by shame, guilt, fear, doubt, and condemnation.

When you focus on your brokenness, rather than celebrate your completeness, you live life on the treadmill of regret, which causes a lifestyle of self-devaluation, self-sabotage, self-rejection, and self-punishment.

Take a few minutes and see if you can identify how you live in regret instead of wholeness. Look for patterns of negative thinking; those negative recordings that play in your mind when you make a mistake or start believing God for something better in your life.

_____

_____

_____

_____

_____

_____

_____

_____

What would it be like if those thoughts were replaced by what God says about you?

_____

_____

_____

_____

_____

"Catching yourself in the act," is a phrase I use in my classes to help people become more aware of their thoughts, behaviors, and patterns. It's not just about figuring out what has wounded you, or what pushes your buttons. It means living in the present, allowing yourself to experience the moment, and then making a conscious decision as to how you want to experience the moment.

Perfect practice makes perfect

Think back to an experience that you wished you had handled differently. Now replay it in your imagination and practice how you would have liked to have handled the situation. Practice it over and over in your mind, like an athlete practices the skill he/she wants to perform on the playing field. As you practice you create a new experience or pathway in the brain, you are renewing your mind.

_____

_____

_____

_____

_____

Change your story, and you can change your life.

Is there a story that you tell over and over to other people or yourself? Are you the victim? Everyone has stories; they are filled with the experiences and mysteries of life throughout childhood. Your experiences, and the way you remember them, shapes what you believe about yourself and how you view the world. When you relive your story as a victim, you create an environment for victimization. You can rewrite your story by creating a new ending.

What happened to you may not have been your fault, but healing from the wounds of the past is your responsibility.

How would you like to change the ending to your story? Imagine that you are sitting in a movie theater watching the story of your life; no one is there but you. You see the people and circumstances; you remember how it always ends.

Now, picture the screen going to that gray static and visualize rewriting your ending. Picture the way you want it to end—not as a victim but as a victor. You can't change what has happened to you, but you can change what you do with the experience. Take some time and rewrite your end to a past experience.

_____

_____

_____

_____

_____

_____

_____

_____

_____

_____

_____

CHAPTER 3

The Case of a Hijacked Identity

In the previous chapter, I addressed the case of a false identity. A false identity is one we adopt as a result of our experiences. In this chapter, I will examine how our identity can be hijacked. The word hijacked is used when someone takes something over. Our car gets hijacked, our emotions can get hijacked, and our identity can get hijacked.

A case of religious hijacking

He (Jesus) told his next story to some who were complacently pleased with themselves over their moral performance and looked down their noses at the common people: "Two men went up to the Temple to pray, one a Pharisee, the other a tax man. The Pharisee posed and prayed like this: 'Oh,

God, I thank you that I am not like other people — robbers, crooks, adulterers, or, heaven forbid, like this tax man. I fast twice a week and tithe on all my income.'

13 "Meanwhile the tax man, slumped in the shadows, his face in his hands, not daring to look up, said, 'God, give mercy. Forgive me, a sinner.'"

14 Jesus commented, "This tax man, not the other, went home made right with God. If you walk around with your nose in the air, you're going to end up flat on your face, but if you're content to be simply yourself, you will become more than yourself." (Luke 18: 9-12 The Message)

The Pharisees were known for their religious piety. It is easy to get hijacked by religion when our identity is based on performance and keeping the rules. Consequently, religion keeps us in fear, shame, and guilt, hijacking our true identity.

A case of personal hijacking

The following list is a few of the ways we get hijacked:

-I don't pray enough.

-I pray more than others.

-I don't read my Bible enough.

-I read my Bible more than others.

-I don't go to church enough.

-I go to church more than others.

While all of us could improve in these areas, our identity is not based on how much or how little we pray, read the Bible or go to church. Our identity is discovered in our relationship with Christ. When our identity is based on our performance, we are not in a relationship. We are in bondage.

Can you make a list of ways you may be hijacked in your identity?

_____

_____

_____

_____

_____

A case of the self-made man/woman hijacking

"The farm of a certain rich man produced a terrific crop. He talked to himself: 'What can I do? My barn isn't big enough for this harvest.' Then he said, 'Here is what I'll do: I'll tear down my barns and build bigger ones. Then I'll gather in all my grain and goods, and I'll say to myself, Self, you've done well! You've got it made and can now retire. Take it easy and have the time of your life!'

20 "Just then God showed up and said, 'Fool! Tonight you die. And your barn full of goods—who gets it?'

21 "That's what happens when you fill your barn with Self and not with God."(Luke 12:16-21 The Message)

While this story seems extreme, it is told to show us that our identity is not in our success. God wants us to be successful, but neither our success nor our failures identify how God created us. The farmer made his success all about him and his identity. If we do not have a strong sense of self, we will allow our success and failures to hijack our identity.

You may have a great job, own your own successful business, or have an important position in your community, but that is not your identity.

Have you allowed success or failures to identify you? If so how? Take a moment and be honest with yourself, and list any successes or failures that you have allowed to affect how you see yourself.

Success:

_____

_____

_____

_____

_____

_____

Failures:

_____

_____

_____

_____

_____

_____

_____

Note: You are not your mistakes or successes. Just because you messed up doesn't mean you are a mess up. You may have an addiction, but that is not your identity. Don't allow mistakes, addictions, or successes to hijack your true identity.

A case of parental hijacking

Sandra was a competent young woman struggling with her identity. Her dad, a successful businessperson, insisted that she go to college and get a degree in business. While this was not her passion, she wanted to please her dad and believed that he had her best interest at heart. She struggled with her college course, not because she couldn't do the work but because she had no interest. She dropped out of school and took a minimum wage job and struggled with what she wanted to do. When asked the question, "What would you do if you could do anything you wanted?" She said, she wanted to go to a vocational school. Dad apologized for trying to make his daughter into his image and agreed to pay for her schooling. Today, she is successfully growing her business.

Parents want the best for their children and often want them to follow in their footsteps. Some will go as far as to impose their will on to their child, as it relates to education and vocations. When parental guidance is coupled with the passion, purpose and destiny of their children, the maximum result is accomplished.

However, when the will of the parents is imposed on the future of their children without consideration of the passion and purpose of the child, there may be a parental identity hijacking.

I have worked with young and older adults who were trying to please parents by following the family business or profession only to find out they had no passion for what they were doing. This often leaves a trail of unfinished college degrees, failed businesses, depression, and strained relationships. It is not my intention to make parents sound bad. I am a parent and know that my intentions have always been what I thought was in the best interest of my children. However, with the best of intentions, we often fail to consider the passion, purpose, and destiny of our children.

Successful but depressed:

I heard of a man who became a successful surgeon to please his father. After years of practice and chronic depression, he gave up his profession to fulfill his passion. What was it? He always wanted to be a long distance truck driver.

Can you relate to a hijacked Identity, if so how?

_____

_____

_____

_____

_____

_____

Here is a tough question: Can you relate to trying to make your child into your image? If so how?

_____

_____

_____

_____

A case of educational hijacking:

Did you take a vocational aptitude evaluation in school? I remember taking one in the latter part of elementary school. I was told that I would need to find a vocation working with my hands. The way my mind translated that information was that I did not have the intelligence to do anything else. Consequently, I took the road of least resistance during my school years and thought there was no reason for me to go to college. While working with your hands is an admirable vocation, the truth is, I wasn't very good at it. It was later in life that I discovered a different path and advanced my education.

My point is: we can become hijacked by the world around us. This is the message of

Romans 12:2: "Don't let the world around you squeeze (hijack) you into its mold..." J. B. Phillips Translation.

Can you think of a case where you may have been hijacked by the world around you?

_____

_____

_____

_____

_____

_____

_____

Can you identify any limiting beliefs that you have about your abilities?

_____

_____

_____

_____

_____

_____

_____

What limiting beliefs are hindering you from moving forward?

_____

_____

_____

_____

_____

_____

_____

How would your life be different without those limiting beliefs? This is the work of transformation, "renewing the mind."

_____

_____

_____

_____

_____

_____

_____

Who would you be without the limiting
beliefs?

_____

_____

_____

_____

_____

_____

_____

What steps are you willing to take to
remove any limiting beliefs?

_____

_____

_____

_____

_____

_____

_____

_____

CHAPTER 4

The Identity Sniper

A sniper is an assassin that waits in the shadows—with a long-range rifle—ready to take out its target with a single shot. The victim is not aware of the presence of the shooter. The enemy of our identity, Satan, lurks in the shadows of our lives, ready to take us out at any given moment. His high-velocity weapon is REJECTION.

The seeds of rejection are planted in our hearts and minds at an early age, sometimes while in our mother's wombs. When the fear of rejection rules our lives, we become an easy target. Here is a short list of the causes of the feeling of rejection:

-An unwanted pregnancy

-The loss of a parent, through death or divorce

-The absence of a parent, through illness, job displacement or military deployment

-Separation from parents due to long-term infant illness

-Physical abuse

-Sexual abuse

-Emotional abuse

-Verbal abuse

-Conflicts between parents

-Unstable home environment

-Lack of peer acceptance

-Abandonment

-Adoption

-Placement in foster care

-Our childhood perception of events

The list could go on and on, but I think you get the point. Almost anything can plant seeds of rejection. Rejection is the most powerful weapon the enemy can use against us. We can be on top of the world one moment, and one negative word or a disapproving glance from someone whose approval we seek can destroy our confidence, makeing us question our true worth and value.

The most common way that we learn to deal with rejection is by getting other people's approval. We are social beings, and desire to have the love, acceptance, and approval of others. As children, we often take on the responsibility for adult behavior. In others words, a child may think: *if I am good enough the negative behavior of my parents or adults, in my life, will change.* Consequently, you may have become a people pleaser attempting to control other people's behavior, which most often results in more feelings of rejection. Unfortunately, rejection—and/or the perception of rejection—are a fact of life. Learning to deal with it, in a positive way, is the result of a transformed mind.

Take some time and identify ways in which you have experienced rejection. I am providing extra space for this exercise; take your time, this list will be used later in this self-coaching process.

_____

_____

_____

_____

_____

_____

_____

_____

_____

_____

_____

_____

_____

_____

Good News:

Your experience of rejection does not go unnoticed by your heavenly Father. Before

Jesus was born, it was foretold that He would know how you feel.

"He was despised and rejected and forsaken by men, a Man of sorrows and pains, and acquainted with grief and sickness; and like one from whom men hide their faces. He was despised, and we did not appreciate His worth or have any esteem for Him." Isa 53:3

Read this passage in the message translation:

The servant grew up before God—a scrawny seedling, a scrubby plant in a parched field. There was nothing attractive about him, nothing to cause us to take a second look. He was looked down on and passed over, a man who suffered, who knew pain firsthand.

(You may be able to identify with this description of Jesus.)

One look at him and people turned away. We looked down on him, thought he was scum. But the fact is, it was our pains he carried— our disfigurements, all the things wrong with us. We thought he brought it on himself, that God was punishing him for his own failures. But it was our sins that did that to him, that ripped and tore and crushed him—our sins!

He took the punishment, and that made us whole.

Through his bruises we get healed. We're all like sheep who've wandered off and gotten lost. We've all done our own thing, gone our own way. And God has piled all our sins, everything we've done wrong, on him. Isaiah 53:3-6 The Message (MSG)

Make a list of the ways that you can identify with this description of Jesus. If you see yourself in this portrait it is because it *is* you.

_____

_____

_____

_____

_____

_____

He took on our human condition. He experienced your rejection so that He would know your pain and show you how to overcome and be free of the pain, fear and, destructive behavior caused by rejection. Without a positive way of dealing with the negative emotions associated with rejection, you will experience anxiety, depression, anger, fear, and loss of your true identity.

How do you generally respond to rejection?

_____

_____

_____

_____

_____

_____

Rejection is painful at every level. The fact that rejection is a fact of life doesn't make it right or acceptable to be rejected or for us to reject others. However, there is no such thing as a rejection blocker.

A new paradigm

Go back to the list that you created earlier, the one about your experiences of rejection.

Rather than deny the experience; allow yourself to feel the pain. It is normal to have negative feelings about the experience of rejection. You have to give yourself time to process your emotions. While "moving on" is important, if you "move on" without processing the experience, you will relive it at another time in your life. As you experience the pain of rejection, make sure you are breathing deeply; calm your heart and still your mind.

Note: Acknowledging the pain does not give you permission to be destructive to yourself or others.

Now write down how you have responded in the past. Now you can rewrite the memory to fit how you would like to respond. This creates a new path in your brain, a new way of thinking.

First, the way you have responded in the past.

_____

_____

_____

_____

_____

_____

_____

_____

_____

_____

Secondly, clear your mind of any negative emotions by talking with a trusted friend, writing down your feelings, breathing deeply, and practicing the new way to respond. These methods can help clear your mind.

_____

_____

_____

_____

_____

_____

_____

_____

Thirdly, avoid the victim mentality. It's easy to fall into this trap of believing that you were treated unfairly, that you were taken advantage of, or that people are prejudice. Okay, let's admit that these things happen. Sometimes it's the other way, and we weren't the person for the job, or the relationship wasn't the fit for us. There are many reasons people get rejected. The point is not why you were rejected; the point is, what are you going to do? What is your next step? Are you going to be a victim and sit on the sidelines of life, bitter and broken, or find a way to be victorious?

How are you presently responding to rejection?

_____

_____

_____

_____

_____

_____

_____

How would you like to respond to rejection?

_____

_____

_____

_____

_____

_____

What steps would you like to put in place to deal with the next experience of rejection?

_____

_____

_____

_____

_____

_____

_____

CHAPTER 5

Shame, The Black Mark on Our Identity and The Stain on Our Soul.

While it is not my intent, in this self-coaching study, to write a book about shame, this chapter may be the most powerful and difficult in this process. This chapter deals with the most intimate secrets and destructive self-imaginations of our lives. Shame is the black mark on our identities and the stain on our souls.

Shame is different than the Identity sniper. Shame is ever present, constantly playing in the back of our minds. Shame tells us who we could have been or should have been. Shame tells us who we can't be, but never tells us our true identity. Shame is often imposed on us. "Shame on you" colors in the black mark of our identity.

Shame is universal. All of us experience it at some level. I have dealt with the rich that were ashamed of their wealth; the poor who are ashamed of their poverty. I have worked with thin people who are ashamed of their bodies and obese people who are ashamed of their weight. Shame lies in wait in the shadows of our thoughts, tainting how we see ourselves and how we believe the world sees us. Shame shows up in our appearance, our body image, family, parenting, money, work, health, addictions, sex, and aging. My point is that shame can show up anywhere.

As painful as this may be, take a few minutes and identify any points of shame that you may have in your life.

_____

_____

_____

_____

_____

_____

_____

The source of shame

Shame is often imposed: who of us has not heard or used the phrase "Shame on you?" Shame is caused by what has been done to you. The actions of others can bring shame: abuse, rejection, sexual abuse, rape, loss of a job or position. A perceived failure to "measure up" can induce a feeling of shame. Then there are our own actions or behaviors that bring shame to our lives. Who of us has not said something that we were ashamed of saying? Maybe our actions harmed someone and, consequently, we are ashamed of our behavior.

Note: Remember this is just for you, so be honest with yourself. You may want to use a separate sheet of paper for this if you are doing this study with a group.

Now reflecting back to your points of shame. Can you identify the source of your shame?

_____

_____

_____

_____

_____

_____

_____

How are any of these points of shame affecting your relationship with God?

_____

_____

_____

_____

_____

_____

How are your points of shame affecting your relationship with others?

_____

_____

_____

_____

_____

_____

_____

How are your points of shame affecting what you want out of life?

_____

_____

_____

_____

_____

_____

_____

_____

I know of no other way to deal with shame outside of the work of salvation. Where do we put it? Who takes it for us? How do we get cleansed from our shame, even if it was our fault? The words of an old hymn ask the question and then answers it for us.

What can wash away my sin (shame)?

Nothing but the blood of Jesus;

What can make me whole again?

Nothing but the blood of Jesus.

(Refrain)

Oh! precious is the flow

That makes me white as snow;

No other fount I know,

Nothing but the blood of Jesus.

For my pardon, this I see,

Nothing but the blood of Jesus;

For my cleansing this my plea,

Nothing but the blood of Jesus.

(Refrain)

Nothing can for sin atone,

Nothing but the blood of Jesus;

Naught of good that I have done,

Nothing but the blood of Jesus.

(Refrain)

This is all my hope and peace,

Nothing but the blood of Jesus;

This is all my righteousness,
Nothing but the blood of Jesus.
(Refrain)
Now by this I'll overcome—
Nothing but the blood of Jesus,
Now by this I'll reach my home—
Nothing but the blood of Jesus.
(Refrain)
Glory! Glory! This I sing—
Nothing but the blood of Jesus,
All my praise for this I bring—
Nothing but the blood of Jesus.

First, Shame needs a healing voice. The secrecy of shame breeds emotional toxicity, which affects the way we see the world and the way we think the world see us. We are looking through the stained spot of our identity. Giving shame a voice brings it out of the shadows into the light.

Take a few moments and "tell it to Jesus." Writing it is an effective way of giving the pain of shame a healing voice. I recommend that you use a separate sheet of paper so that you can dispose of it, if you would like. Once you have given your pain a voice, then you can do the work of forgiving yourself and others.

Note: We are often pushed into forgiveness prematurely. Forgiveness is important, but premature forgiveness doesn't take the stain away.

Read through this passage of Scripture slowly. Let it speak to you.

"The Spirit of the Lord God is upon Me,

Because the Lord has anointed Me

To preach good tidings to the poor;

He has sent Me to heal the brokenhearted,

To proclaim liberty to the captives,

And the opening of the prison to those who are bound;

2

To proclaim the acceptable year of the Lord,

And the day of vengeance of our God;

To comfort all who mourn,

3

To console those who mourn in Zion,

To give them beauty for ashes,

The oil of joy for mourning,

The garment of praise for the spirit of heaviness;

That they may be called trees of righteousness,

The planting of the Lord, that He may be glorified."

4

And they shall rebuild the old ruins,

They shall raise up the former desolations,

And they shall repair the ruined cities,

The desolations of many generations.

.5

Strangers shall stand and feed your flocks,

And the sons of the foreigner

Shall be your plowmen and your vinedressers.

6

But you shall be named the priests of the Lord,

They shall call you the servants of our God.

You shall eat the riches of the Gentiles,

And in their glory you shall boast.

7

Instead of your shame you shall have double honor,

And instead of confusion they shall rejoice in their portion.

Therefore in their land they shall possess double;

Everlasting joy shall be theirs. Isaiah 61: 1-7 New King James Version (NKJV)

What is the Holy Spirit saying to you?

_____

_____

_____

_____

_____

_____

How will your life be different without the stain of shame?

_____

_____

_____

_____

_____

_____

_____

What will your life be like if you don't give your shame to Jesus?

_____

_____

_____

_____

_____

_____

_____

What action steps do you want to take to give Jesus your shame?

_____

_____

_____

_____

_____

_____

_____

_____

_____

CHAPTER 6

Restoring Your True Identity Through Your Passion, Purpose and Personality

The world is big on recreating or reinventing yourself. Public relations firms charge large fees to reinvent politicians, celebrities, agencies, and even corporations. Our identity in Christ is not something we create. It is something we discover and nurture. As stated in a previous chapter, Paul told us not to let the world give us our identity.

"And do not be conformed to this world, but be transformed by the renewing of your mind, that you may prove what is that good and acceptable and perfect will of God." (Romans 12:2 NKJV)

The J. B. Phillips says it this way:

"Don't let the world around you squeeze you into its own mold, but let God re-mold your minds from within, so that you may prove in

practice that the plan of God for you is good, meets all his demands and moves towards the goal of true maturity."

The idea of "re-molding" or "transforming" suggests that what was created has become something other than it was intended to be. The message of the Bible is about restoration, renewing, and redeeming. The truth is you were not created in a vacuum. You were born with a purpose, passion, and destiny.

Oh yes, you shaped me first inside, then out;

you formed me in my mother's womb.

I thank you, High God—you're breathtaking!

Body and soul, I am marvelously made!

I worship in adoration—what a creation!

You know me inside and out, you know every bone in my body; You know exactly how I was made, bit by bit,

how I was sculpted from nothing into something.

Like an open book, you watched me grow from conception to birth; all the stages of my life were spread out before you,

The days of my life all prepared before I'd even lived one day. Psalms 139: 13-16

David was given this marvelous insight that humanity is not a biological accident or a product of genetics emerging out of a world of chaos. You were created with a purpose and destiny that your soul longs to discover. The New Testament version of this truth is sighted at the beginning of this self-coaching study.

It's in Christ that we find out who we are and what we are living for. Long before we first heard of Christ and got our hopes up, he had his eye on us, had designs on us for glorious living, part of the overall purpose he is working out in everything and everyone. (Ephesians 1:11-12: The Message)

Take a moment and write down your thoughts as you read these scriptures.

What do you hear God saying to you in your spirit?

_____

_____

_____

_____

_____

_____

_____

How could you apply the truth of these scriptures to your life today?

_____

_____

_____

_____

_____

_____

_____

_____

_____

What difference would it make in your life if you embrace the truths of these scriptures?

_____

_____

_____

_____

_____

_____

_____

_____

What impact will it have on you if you do not embrace the truths of these scriptures?

_____

_____

_____

_____

_____

_____

_____

_____

_____

Discovering your passion:

Our passions show up in childhood and can be seen as a window to your purpose and an identity marker. Future teachers will often play school. Future preachers will play church. I love watching our worship leader's youngest son during worship at CFTN. From about two years of age, you could see him passionately absorbed in the worship. His grandparents tell me how he sits at the piano and pretends to write songs, making notes with his pencil, correcting mistakes and then singing his song to whoever will listen. No one is coaching him to do this; it is out of his heart and how God has created him. It's not hard to see the purpose and destiny in a person.

I recently asked a group of civil engineers what they played with as children. One of the men spoke up and talked about his passion for building things, playing with an erector set and building blocks, anything he could use to build something.

Take some time and think back to your childhood passions. Was there anything that stands out to you that may have been a window to your future purpose?

_____

_____

_____

_____

_____

Finding our purpose is often perceived to be mystical, super-spiritual, something outside us, an external manifestation of God's presence. While such expressions of God do occur, they are not the measure of our identity. Since purpose and identity are so closely tied together, it follows that we should be looking for our identity on the inside rather than the outside. Looking for those moments when we feel most alive.

These moments of being alive have a profound place in your memories. They are more powerful, vivid, and impactful than other memories. This is because those moments of being alive are connected with your purpose, your calling, and the nature of God within us.

When have you felt most alive, empowered, energized, productive and creative?

_____

_____

_____

_____

_____

_____

_____

_____

_____

As we mature in our walk with God, we discover that the ordinary is actually extraordinary. Then we can stop chasing some external "supernatural experience" and live out of the supernatural within us. Romans 12:1, in The Message Translation, give us some insight in how to experience the extraordinary life in the everyday living.

"Take your everyday, ordinary life – your sleeping, eating, going-to-work, and walking-around life – and place it before God as an offering. Embracing what God does for you is the best thing you can do for him."

Take a few moments and name all the little things for which you can be thankful.

_____

_____

_____

_____

_____

_____

_____

_____

_____

_____

_____

_____

Clues to your purpose

Take some time and answer the following questions, there is no right or wrong answers. This exercise is to get you thinking about clues to your purpose.

What attracts people to you?

_____

_____

_____

_____

_____

_____

_____

_____

_____

_____

What support or advice do they seek from you?

_____

_____

_____

_____

_____

What areas of life are most interesting to you?

_____

_____

_____

_____

_____

What kind of books do you read?

_____

_____

_____

_____

_____

Are there special scriptures that catch your attention?

_____

_____

_____

_____

_____

Is there a general theme to your favorite
Scriptures?

_____

_____

_____

_____

_____

When do you have the most energy?

_____

_____

_____

_____

_____

What activity causes you to lose track of
time?

_____

_____

_____

_____

_____

What could you do forever?

_____

_____

_____

_____

_____

The work of the Holy Spirit is to attract—silently into our lives things—people and the understanding we need to fulfill our God-given purpose. When we learn to pay attention, take notice, and give ourselves the time to experience these moments—we feel truly alive!

As you look over your responses to these questions, look for patterns that point you toward your purpose and destiny.

_____

_____

_____

_____

_____

_____

_____

_____

_____

_____

Keys to the process

1. <u>Stay open and thankful for what you already have:</u>

Gratitude is the elasticity of the soul, the more you exercise it, the greater its capacity to receive. To live in regret for what we don't have, didn't do, or wish had done is to focus on our lack of potential and purpose. It causes us to lose sight of the abundance of our potential and limits our imagination of what is possible. The wisdom of the Psalmist was his continual focus on giving thanks. He never allowed mistakes and regrets to be the measure of his future.

The attitude or spirit of ungratefulness, which is often manifested by bitterness, anger, grudges, and regret, releases negative energy into our physical bodies that sabotages our ability to unlock doors to our purpose and potential. Yes, what you allow yourself to think about and the emotions you allow yourself to experience, even influences how your mind functions and your physical body operates.

Dr. Bruce Lipton states, *"...our new understanding of the universe's mechanics shows us how the physical body can be directly affected by the immaterial mind. Thoughts, (attitudes, my word) the minds energy, directly influence how the physical brain controls the body's physiology. Thought 'energy' can activate or inhibit the cell's function-producing proteins in the mechanics of constructive and destructive interference."*

If we understand that our negative thoughts and attitudes (a thought connected to an emotion) consumes energy as much as physical efforts, we will gain insight into our fatigue and lack of motivation. When we change our attitude from one of regret, anger, and bitterness and develop an attitude of gratefulness, we actually gain energy instead of burn it:

Psalm 92:1, It is a good thing to give thanks unto the Lord, and to sing praises unto thy name, O Most High (KJV).

Psalm 107:1, O give thanks unto the LORD, for he is good: for his mercy endureth forever (KJV).

Is there a negative attitude that you would like to let go of?

_____

_____

_____

_____

_____

_____

_____

What would be the positive result of letting go of this negative attitude?

_____

_____

_____

_____

_____

What would the result be if you did not let go of this negative attitude?

_____

_____

_____

_____

_____

_____

_____

What steps are you ready to take to let go of any negative attitude?

_____

_____

_____

_____

_____

_____

_____

_____

_____

_____

_____

2. Trust the process:

Patience is the virtue everyone would like to have, but no one wants to wait for. When we move from an attitude and lifestyle of regret, bitterness, and grudge holding, we want to see immediate results. I am often asked, "How long does it take to make life changes?" My response is, "You can't hurry growth, but you can slow it down." Then I remind them to "trust the process."

Learning the patience and wisdom of a farmer can help us through this process. The seasoned farmer knows the process of tilling the ground, fertilizing, planting, and watering his potential crop. He knows the seed he planted; he knows the soil and the climate, and he leaves nothing to chance. He understands there are seasons of planting and seasons of waiting, before the season of reaping. He knows the insects and other crop destroyers to watch for, and he defends his potential harvest. When patience is based on knowledge, it is much more effective. When we know the seeds we plant; our vision, purpose, and destiny and then nurture it with the right "fertilizer" of thoughts, books, seminars, training, etc. we are preparing for our harvest.

I tell my seminar students, "I can pretty well tell you where you will be five years from now by the books you're reading and the teachers you are listening to." If we are not tilling the soil of our minds, planting seeds for growth, nurturing and watering our dreams and destiny we will not have a harvest:

James 5:7-9 – "... You see farmers do this all the time, waiting for their valuable crops to mature, patiently letting the rain do its slow but sure work. Be patient like that. Stay steady and strong..."(MSG).

What seeds are you planting for your future?

What books are you reading? What classes are you taking?

What goals have you set?

_____

_____

_____

_____

_____

_____

_____

_____

_____

_____

_____

_____

In what kind of soil (attitude) are you planting these seeds?

Is it positive or negative soil, the soil of gratitude, soil of hope?

What needs to be removed from the soil? Is it filled with fear, regret, complaints, bitterness, etc.?

_____

_____

_____

_____

_____

_____

_____

_____

_____

_____

3. Avoid the 'victim mentality.'

When I confronted one of my students about using victim language, she retorted, "I AM the victim!" With a few exceptions such as rape, crimes committed against us, and pre-volitional abuse (child abuse), etc. we volunteer for most of our abuse. Regardless of its cause, in all cases of victimization, there comes a point when we have to take responsibility for our healing. When we complain about something we are not willing to do anything about, we are playing the victim. When we continually blame other people for chronic negative circumstances, we are playing the victim.

Victim language always has a negative qualifier: *I don't have enough education, I didn't go to the right school, I didn't get a chance for life, I was abused, etc.* These things may all be true, but what happened to you is not the biggest problem. The larger issue is what you allow it to do to you. The victim mentality can become our excuse for remaining in our present circumstances.

Many books have been written, movies made, and stories told about those who overcame their abusive past, and the one thing they all have in common is the overcomer had to make peace with their past to claim their future.

The Scriptures state that when we understand God's love for us, we are empowered to overcome every kind of life challenge:

Romans 8:37, No, in all these things we win an overwhelming victory through him who has proved his love for us (J. B. Phillips Translation).

All of us struggle with the victim mentality from time to time.

Is there any area of your life where you are in the victim mode?

_____

_____

_____

_____

_____

_____

What would be the result if you let go of the victim mentality?

_____

_____

_____

_____

_____

_____

What will be the result if you don't let go of the victim mentality?

_____

_____

_____

_____

_____

_____

_____

_____

4. Listen to the Holy Spirit:

Each one of us carries on a continual internal dialogue with ourselves. This intrapersonal conversation is generally the internalization of our parent or caregiver's voice. It's like a tape recorder going off in our minds when something triggers old thought patterns. We make a mistake, and the tape player goes off, "You can't do anything right;" "You're an idiot;" "You will never amount to anything," and so forth. These pre-programmed, internalized thoughts keep us from unlocking our purpose. These thoughts and statements must be replaced with new, positive affirmations that become a part of our new thought process. When we learn to listen to the voice of our Creator, we begin to understand the difference between our voice, other peoples' voices or opinions, and the guiding voice of the Holy Spirit. However, His voice can be drowned out by our lack of understanding of God and who

He is in our lives and by erroneous theology. (Refer to the chapter on "mistaken identity.")

Which voice are you listening to, the condemning, judgmental, shaming voices of the flesh, or the encouraging, uplifting, empowering voice of the Holy Spirit?

Isaiah 58:11, I will always guide you. I will satisfy your needs in a land that is baked by the sun. I will make you stronger. You will be like a garden that has plenty of water. You will be like a spring whose water never runs dry (NIRV).

Isaiah 58:11 (The Message): If you get rid of unfair practices, quit blaming victims, quit gossiping about other people's sins, if you are generous with the hungry and start giving yourselves to the down-and-out, your lives will begin to glow in the darkness, your shadowed lives will be bathed in sunlight. I will always show you where to go. I'll give you a full life in the emptiest of places—firm muscles, strong bones. You'll be like a well-watered garden, a gurgling spring that never runs dry.

How do you know the difference between the voice of the Holy Spirit and the voice of the flesh?

_____

_____

_____

_____

_____

_____

_____

_____

Romans 8: 1-2 No condemnation now hangs over the head of those who are "in" Jesus Christ. For the new spiritual principle of life "in" Christ lifts me out of the old vicious circle of sin and death.

3-4 The Law never succeeded in producing righteousness—the failure was always the weakness of human nature. But God has met this by sending his own Son Jesus Christ to live in that human nature which causes the trouble. And, while Christ was actually taking upon himself the sins of men, God condemned that sinful nature. So that we are able to meet the Law's requirements, so long as we are living no longer by the dictates of our sinful nature, but in obedience to the promptings of the Spirit. J.B. Phillips New Testament (PHILLIPS)

5. Move toward your goal rather than away:

Have you ever made the statement, "I will never..." and find yourself doing the very thing you never thought you would do? I can remember saying that I would never move to Arizona. In spite of that Sharon (my wife) and I moved here in 1989 and my time here has proved to be the most productive years of our lives. Our 'point of resistance' may be an indicator of our purpose and calling. I am not just talking about where we live or work, your 'point of resistance' maybe the people you avoid.

One of my students found herself working with a group of people she always shunned, in a nice way of course. Once she moved beyond her 'point of resistance,' she found joy and relationships she never knew were possible. It's not that her life was bad before; to the contrary, her life was very good, but in her words, "It has gone from good to great." We need to understand how the Holy Spirit works. He is the great alchemist; He takes all the things in our life, mixes them together, and brings forth something new and better.

Paul the great writer, teacher and leader knew that growth is always about going beyond our current boundaries:

Philippians 3:14, I'm not saying that I have this all together, that I have it made. But I am well on my way, reaching out for Christ, who has so wondrously reached out for me. Friends, don't get me wrong: By no means do

I count myself an expert in all of this, but I've got my eye on the goal, where God is beckoning us onward—to Jesus. I'm off and running and I'm not turning back (The Message).

Take a few minutes and write what you have gained from this process.

Do you have a better understanding of who you are?

_____

_____

_____

_____

_____

_____

What steps are you ready to take?

_____

_____

_____

_____

_____

_____

This self-study guide is simply a tool to help discover your identity in Christ. If you want or need further assistance, Life Impact LLC has well trained, certified Christian life coaches that can facilitate your growth process. **The world doesn't need less of you; it needs more of God that is in you.**

58788036R00055

Made in the USA
Charleston, SC
19 July 2016